About the author

Cindy is a christian, an entrepreneur, a daughter, a sister, and a friend. She holds a Bachelor's of Business Administration, and an MSc in Business Economics. As both a christian and a business consultant she has found that most business's struggle either due to the owners limited understanding of how the spirit realm works or due to lack of knowledge on what to do as business owners. The steps highlighted in this book are both business and faith driven.

Summary

This book is a christian guide on how to do business. We therefore look at business in two ways i.e. through internal and external business influencers. Some of the internal influencers we look at include: the business owners motive for starting the business, the impact of the business on the environment, timing, the business owners personal traits, skill set, the impact of the business in the community as a whole, etc. The external influencers we look at include: infrastructural development both in transport and information technology, government infrastructure, educational infrastructure, cultural influence etc.

CHAPTER ONE

For as long as humanity has been in existence demand and supply have created very interesting dynamics in the economy. It doesn't matter in what part of the world you are from, when demand exceeds supply there is an opportunity to trade. But in this book we learn that this is not enough. Many developed economies have digital platforms upon which they can effectively carry out e-commerce. But in the less developed economies we find that businesses have relied more on physical market places where buyers meet sellers in person to carry out trade.

The core concept of this business guide has been designed around biblical principles. These principles worked for people in the Bible and continue to work for different people today. In many parts of the world you will find that christians for one reason or another fail to do business. This could be because:

They lack knowledge. They do not know that most things happen in the spiritual realm before they happen in the physical, and have therefore relied on their own strength and not that of the Lord.

They lack understanding. Whereas some may have the biblical knowledge. Most of them lack the understanding on how to use the biblical word to win especially when facing challenges in their businesses.

Some have been misled by false prophets or people using the word of God to their own advantage. This has caused christians in business to either give up or get frustrated in the long run.

Some are lazy. God wants us to go out and actively seek Him with all our strength and might. But at the same time He wants us to work hard at everything. Take for example Jacob who later became Israel. He did not sit back while passively waiting for Esau to forego his blessing as a first born son of the family. Rather he actively pursued it. For Jacob getting a wife was a struggle, marriage was a struggle, because the wife he loved failed to have children for a longtime. He fought to leave his father in laws house. He also wrestled with an angel to go back to his ancestral village. Eventually Jacob won, and became Israel. So all the Christian Faith refers to Israel the nation as chosen because Jacob fought. So in order to get into the full blessing of the

Lord one has to fight for it. For it is also written that the kingdom of God suffers violence and the violent take it by force.

Some christians are still under ancestral bondage. This is especially common in christians who either lack the knowledge or understanding of the word. Most of us are familiar with the way God called Abraham. Out of his father's house and out of the nation he was accustomed to. This is because clearly Abraham neither came from a God fearing nation nor family. So God needed Abraham to leave behind his ancestral beliefs so that he could walk into his blessing. Same thing applies in business. Most individuals are clueless or have a clear lack of knowledge of the practices and beliefs of their ancestors. Many of our ancestors made deals with the devil to hoard wealth. These covenants they made were actually binding from generation to generation, and because at a certain point a specific generation stops worshipping these demons. The demons resort to torturing them. They sometimes cause poverty. Other times they cause early death. They can also cause drunk ness. These demons have actually led to slavery in many parts of the world, and have resulted in bondage of certain communities into everlasting seasons of lack.

In other cases these demons seek to create uniformity. That means that if your ancestors only made 10 dollars daily from year to year. Then this will also become your life. If your ancestors never started businesses but you do. Then the covenants they made will bring you into the same uniformity.

Some christians do not have enough faith to move their mountains. You see as a business owner you are faced with many challenges daily. But it's written that even with faith as big as a mustard seed, you could say to the mulberry tree 'Pull yourself up by the roots and plant yourself in the sea' and it would obey you. Remember faith is a gift of the spirit and the Father is always willing to give you whatever you ask for. He loves us more than our earthly parents ever will.

CHAPTER TWO

Relationship with God

Before starting a business it's important to ensure that you are doing a business that is aligned to God's purpose and will for your life. So It's important that we seek help and guidance from the Lord so that we are not wasting our time. It's clearly written in the Bible that we seek first the kingdom of heaven, and all the rest will fall in line. This holds true for businesses as well. Seeking first the kingdom of heaven simply means that one should hunger for a relationship with God before pursuing a business.

You want to think of God as a partner in your business. Like any physical partner you need to get to know them first. The same applies to you and God. Let Him be fully invested in you and you in Him. Look at Job, who was very successful both in his professional and personal life because he was fully committed to God. Job's commitment to God even helped him go through some tough times. Tough times are also in business. Every business in every economy will at some point go through a difficult time. So it's in these times that we need to really know the God we serve.

How one keeps a good relationship with God.

By reading the word of God daily, and meditating on it. Meditation is reflecting on the word of God in application to one's daily life or persistent situation. When starting a business one need not be a lukewarm christian. The bible clearly says that God prefers it when you are either hot or cold. But the lukewarm he spits out. Therefore, waiting for Sunday to commune with God is not an option. Create time, make this your number one priority everyday. Take time off to worship and praise God daily. Acknowledge that without Him you are lost. Tell God about your plans and He will guide your way.

Through prayer and fasting. This has always been the unbeatable combination. David, Daniel, Esther, Jesus Himself and so many other people in the Bible are examples of the power of prayer and fasting. Remember that as a Christian no weapon fashioned against you shall prosper. Also remember that the strongest weapon you have is prayer. You can only communicate with God through prayer. But through prayer and fasting we are able to fight the enemy with bigger weapons leading to breakthrough in most cases. Sometimes if a situation is not changing in prayer we need to fast to get breakthrough results.

How to fast effectively.

Most scholars define fasting as a period of time in which one withholds self from food and drink in a bid to get a response from God in regards to a specific situation. For example some people can fast to get revenue streams, to get funding for a project etc. Biblically the way people fast has evolved greatly from the Old Testament where people literally wore rugs and put dust on their faces during fasting, to a new way in the New Testament. Fasting according to the New Testament requires one to put oil on their head and wash their face, this way it will not be obvious to men. Jesus also emphasized that we need to be aware of the way we treat others, especially during fasting.

How does one pray effectively.

When the disciples asked Jesus to teach them how to pray. He taught them the prayer 'Our Father'. Jesus did not mean this verbatim but it was more of a guidance on how to pray as illustrated below:

Worship (Our Father who art in heaven, Hallowed be thy name).

Based on the prayer 'Our Father' we start out by honoring God in words or songs. It's known that God can do everything and anything, but He cannot worship Himself. As human beings our sole purpose on earth is to worship and praise God. During praise and worship the glory of God manifests. Then He is able to listen to our prayers clearly. It is also important to note that the Lord listens to those who worship Him in spirit and in truth.

Establish a relationship with God. (Thy Kingdom come thy will be done on earth as it is in heaven).

When we ask for the kingdom of God we are asking for a relationship with God. It is clearly written in the Bible that when Jesus went up to heaven he promised to come back and together with God the Father, they are to make a home with those who believe. It is important to remember that we have to pray that the will of God is still fulfilled in our lives despite our own personal needs and wants. For no one knows what tomorrow holds apart from God.

Make your supplications or requests known to God (Give us this day our daily bread).

Before Jesus went to heaven He promised that whatever we asked for in His name He will do so that the name of God the Father will be glorified. It's important to ask God for daily bread not just the physical bread, but also for words nourishing the soul from the Bible. For the Bible also says that man shall not live by bread alone but by every word that proceeds from the mouth of God. So daily we must read the Bible because it's the sword by which we get to fight for physical 'bread'.

The bible also says in Matthew "Ask and it will be given to you; seek and you will find; knock and the door will be opened to you. For everyone who asks receives; he who seeks finds; and to him who knocks, the door will be opened." Therefore do not hesitate to ask God for what you need in your business, for then the door shall be opened unto you.

Seek forgiveness to be forgiven. (Forgive us our trespasses as we forgive those who trespass against us).

As a Christian it is important that you ask God for forgiveness for your sins daily. This way there are no hindrances to our prayers getting to His throne room. Remember the prayers of a sinner are detestable in the eyes of God. It's important to reflect daily on our journey and establish whether it's leading us away or near to God. Also remember that there are things that God hates and are detestable to Him i.e. a heart that rushes to do evil, someone who brings dissension among brothers, a lying tongue to mention but a few.

Pray for protection (Lead us not into temptation but deliver us from every evil).

The Bible says that the devil is like a roaring lion looking for whom to devour. It is also written that the troubles of a righteous man are many but the Lord delivers him from them all. Therefore we need to ask God that He leads our paths away from temptation and sin, thus delivering us from all evil.

As it is written in Ephesians it is important to put on the full armour of Christ so that we can stand against the devil. More often than not as a business owner you will face many challenges. That's why we therefore need:

The Helmet of salvation, by accepting that Jesus Christ died on the cross to save both you and I from sin. Remember the Bible says that Jesus is the way the truth and the life. So no one can go to the Father except through Him. One cannot make decisions when their head is filled with negativity, depression, doubt, despair, anxiety, worry etc. Remember by accepting Jesus Christ as our personal Lord and saviour we are inviting the Holy Spirit into our lives. The Bible says that the Spirit of God is that of a sound mind. Many times people believe that God doesn't talk to them and yet they let the devil speak to them all the time. He brings thoughts of defeat which lead to the above mentioned like anxiety, depression, worrying etc. God is also urgently waiting to talk to you. To give you words of encouragement and not of defeat.

The shield of Faith. The Bible says that faith can move mountains therefore by being faithful in all that we do, we are making it very hard for the arrows of the devil to affect our day to day lives. Think of faith as an offensive weapon against the devil. When your shield is up. The arrows that come flying from witchcraft, sorcery, divination cannot harm you. When in faith you can ward off all evil no matter the plans of the enemy they will not stop you.

The sword which is the word of God. This is the most powerful tool we have as Christians. The Bible clearly says that our weapons are not canal or of this world. The Bible also says that in the beginning was the word and the word was with God and the word became God. It is also well written that the word of God shall not return to Him void, until it has accomplished what it has set out to do. So in order to see business success one has to learn to pray through scripture. Because God is not a man that He should lie if He says it's so, then it's so.

The belt of truth. The belt is what holds the breast plate in place. So when one knows the truth that is written in the word. Then they cannot easily be derailed. They will always stand firm in righteousness knowing what God loves, and what He detests. This way despite the situation the truth will always prevail in their lives.

The breastplate of righteousness. A righteous person is blameless before the eyes of the Lord. The Bible says that many are the troubles of a righteous man but the Lord delivers him from them all. So think of righteousness as protection. Both a helmet and a breastplate protect vital organs of the body. If your head or heart or lungs or kidneys get injured this can disrupt the core of the entire body system. Damage to these organs would greatly deter the way of life of an individual. The same thing applies to life, when one is unrighteous they leave themselves open to attacks from the devil.

The law as it was given to Moses is well laid out in Deuteronomy. As mature christians we are expected to partake in the law. The law is comprehensively written out and isn't limited to just the Ten Commandments as most people might think. As a Christian you must obey, don't create a business that requires you to work on Sunday, for even God rested on the seventh day. A Christian must tithe and offer first fruit for their harvest. Some of the Ten Commandments include; not to steal, not to kill, worship only the one true God, keep the Lord's day holy, do not lie to mention but a few. But most importantly the law in the New Testament requires one to love the Lord their God with all their heart, mind and soul. The bottom line here is to love God more than you love yourself. The other main commandment is to love other people as you love yourself. So in terms of business don't start one that you deem harmful to other people. Just like you would not harm yourself don't bring harm to someone else. For example if you don't drink alcohol, then do not sale alcohol to other people in society.

CHAPTER THREE

Skills and Experience

When starting a business one needs to have the technical capability to run it. Skills can be acquired in two ways either through training or experience. A combination of the two is usually a very big plus. This is not to say that people who have no technical expertise will never be successful in the business of their choice. But many people make the mistake of going into business ventures where they have no technical expertise. This results into an increase in not only their personal stress levels but also creates other unwanted issues like anxiety, depression, or hopelessness. As a result they eventually lose interest in the business all together. Learning a skill is an investment so it's crucial that one learns the in's and outs of the business they are trying to start and grow. We are not saying that an accountant cannot be a Baker, but that there has to be a good balance between skillsman-ship and experience. What we are trying to do is to limit the trial and error period. Because it is a well known fact that time is money. If you want to understand the aspect of your business at every level. It doesn't hurt to first take time to grow your talent and skill by working under someone whom you consider to be an expert in the field this could be in the form of a job, internship, volunteership or fellowship etc.

The best way to start a business therefore is to identify in which areas your expertise lie. Figure out what you are good at and what you want to offer for example a software engineer can set up a coding academy, a pharmacist can set up a pharmacy, a hairstylist can set up a hair salon. A lot of issues can be avoided once one knows the frontend and backend of the business they are starting or running.

Motive for starting the business

There are many reasons as to why people choose to start businesses. But for a business to be successful certain things have to be put into consideration including:

Passion

Passion is such a big motive for doing anything. Many of us may be familiar with the passion of the Christ. This movie is a clear demonstration of how far passion can take us to achieve our goal. We are not saying that you have to die to start a business. But you will probably have to give up a big chunk of your life. Therefore, when starting a business seriously consider how passionate you are about the idea, this is because most businesses do not yield immediate results causing frustration in the beginning, your decision to go on will solely depend on your passion for the project.

To meet a need

Another great motive for starting a business is the realisation of a need in a community and creating a solution to meet that need. For example, realising the need for better medical services can prompt one to setup a medical centre that offers medical services to members of the community.

Profitability

In most business studies this the strongest motive for starting a business. We have to acknowledge that no one starts a business to watch it fail. But it is a well documented fact that many businesses take years without realising profitability. In fact most businesses only become profitable in the long run.

Vocation or Purpose

The truth is that we were all created for a purpose and we therefore recommend this as the biggest motive for starting a business. Every individual is gifted with a calling. A calling is a divine purpose that is beyond daily routine in a bid to earn a living. A divine calling is usually coupled with divine assistance. Sometimes people get called to start up projects that are not necessarily money driven. Examples of search projects include setting up an orphanage, starting a church to minister the word etc

Time

We have looked at the time aspect of business in three basic ways:

When starting a business, it is important that one has the time to run the business. The amount of time one invests will show in the way the business is run and will eventually trickle down into how profitable the business is in the long run. The passion and drive you have for the business will show in the time you dedicate to the business. Do not make the mistake of starting a business if you cannot dedicate time to it daily.

The age at which one starts their business is also very critical and important. Please note that we are not saying that there is a specific age at which one should start a business. But we advise people to start trying out entrepreneurship as early as possible. Although most people prefer to start their businesses in the later stages of their life, this is actually a very dangerous strategy because; the older you are the more susceptible you are to diseases resulting from stress, depression, and pressure due to tense working situations. Younger people are less likely to fall victim to such diseases, and are more likely to adapt quickly while facing tense situations.

Then lastly one needs to be keen in knowing the time to either leave or change the business concept. Most business ideas are wonderful in the beginning but as times changes some things become obsolete. Even the blackberry was once famous, and it had a great customer base. The Iphone which is one of the most famous phone brands evolves annually. So it is very important to know when a business concept either needs to change or when the concept should come to a complete halt. This is to prevent one from making complete losses.

CHAPTER FOUR

There are three types of analysis one has to carry out before running a business successfully:

Self Analysis

This is a detailed examination of one's abilities. Identifying one's strengths and weaknesses. One's personal attributes will go a long way in determining whether they have the ability to start and run a successful business. The attributes we are talking about include;

Leadership

This is a very important aspect in determining whether one has the ability to run a successful business venture. Leadership doesn't mean exercising dominion and power over everyone. But it means being intentional in one's business decisions, knowing how to influence positively the community in and around your business so that you can create value for your company or brand.

Who is a good leader?

A good leader is a good server. This is not only true in the bible but in everyday business applications. Jesus is our example of true leadership. A servant leader relays a positive message to their employees, customers, suppliers, service providers etc. Most stakeholders are more likely to associate with someone who is humble enough to lead as a server and not as a dictator.

A good leader is a visionary.

A visionary is someone who sees the big picture and is able to influence other people to believe in the manifestation of the vision whether in the short or long run. Most successful businesses start out as a dream. But one's ability to not only believe in their dreams but also sale there dream to investors, customers and employers determines one's success story in the business world.

A good leader is decisive.

One of the important qualities of a good leader is the ability to make good decisions, within a given timeframe. With as little information as possible. As a business owner timing is everything, wait too long and you might miss out on an opportunity, react too quickly and you might make a big mistake.

Works well under pressure.

A lot of internal and external pressures arise out of starting and running a business. This therefore requires an individual who works well under pressure and who can make the most out of I'm possible situation with limited information.

Organised and knows how to prioritise.

All business owners must be well organised in order to keep track of their finances, employees, product history etc. This will enable the individual to set priorities on what needs to be handled more urgently than the other.

Good time management skills

A good leader is a good manager of time, as it is often said that time is money, and those who manage their time well have mastered the art of wealth.

Flexible

The best businesses are run by effectual and not causal people, whereas its good to have a business plan. The reality is that a lot will actually happen to your business that was not documented in the business plan, some assumptions drawn in the business plan are unattainable, and therefore you have to be ready for anything and be willing to do whatever it takes within reason to chase your business to success.

Determined or goal orientated.

Successful businesses are started with a goal in mind and in order to reach that goal, the leader has to have unwavering determination that all will be fine. Therefore, a good leader must have a clear destination in terms of a goal the organisation is working towards.

Faithful and Honest/ Straight forward

The backbone of every business is offering genuine products that will create customer loyalty. Once people get what they expect they are more likely to choose your service or product over that of your competitors.

Perseveres and endures

No business grows overnight, especially in the developing economies. More likely than not you will miss something and it will set you back, but fear not because all business owners have been where you are, the only thing that will keep you going in this time is unwavering perseverance and endurance, and you will reap in due time, even the bible says so.

Patient and has self control

A business like anything in life has both ups and downs. Many times in a business someone's patience and self control will be put to the test, especially when dealing with various stakeholders such as employees, shareholders, suppliers, service providers, and in other areas like dealing with your subordinates in a respectful manner that would not make them feel inferior or used in anyway. The line between respect and disrespect is thin therefore and it takes a lot of self control to maintain it.

Market Analysis

After doing extensive research and determining the best opportunities for you to pursue, it's now time to determine if there will be a market for what you have to offer. This could be at International or local markets level. Don't rush into designing expensive marketing advertisements and constructing expensive and complicated business plans before identifying whom you are going to market your product to.

Test the product on the market

After identifying the target market for your product, it is important to test your product out on the target market. This will give you validation that there is actual demand for the product you are trying to offer. Do not make extensive investments before confirming the viability of the market, and it's ability to solve the problem you are trying to solve.

Economic Analysis

This is a critical component in analysing the business as a whole. For any business to thrive, one has to extensively study the economy and the state of other businesses in the economy. Especially the businesses closely related to the one you are going to start.

What is the growth rate of these businesses in terms of market share, how often has the market evolved over the past given period, what impact has the industry had on the economy or community whether negative or positive? Is there potential for growth within the industry given the current economic situation?

It is important to consider the political and legal structure of the country in which you are to carry out your business. This will determine the success and failure of your business in both the long and short run. Don't start an illegal business as this would mean you are breaking the law. But even though the business is operating legally avoid breaking other laws that would ensure the success of your business for example pay your taxes on time, and in the right proportion.

Thank you!

www.ingramcontent.com/pod-product-compliance
Lightning Source LLC
Chambersburg PA
CBHW030543220526
45463CB00007B/2961